BEETLES

TEXT BY ELAINE PASCOE

PHOTOGRAPHS BY DWIGHT KUHN

BLACKBIRCH PRESS, INC.

WOODBRIDGE, CONNECTICUT

Published by Blackbirch Press, Inc.
260 Amity Road
Woodbridge, CT 06525

Email: staff@blackbirch.com
Web site: www.blackbirch.com

Printed in the United States

10 9 8 7 6 5 4 3 2

front cover: Colorado potato beetle
back cover: (left to right) ladybug eggs, ladybug larvae, ladybug larva shedding skin, adult ladybug

Library of Congress Cataloging-in-Publication Data

Pascoe, Elaine.
Beetles / by Elaine Pascoe; photographs by Dwight Kuhn.
       p.   cm. — (Nature close-up)
    Includes bibliographical references (p. 47).
    Summary: Explains the characteristics, habits, life cycle, and appearance of the many species of beetles. Includes experiments.
    ISBN 1-56711-175-0
    1. Beetles—Juvenile literature. 2. Beetles—Experiments—Juvenile literature. [1. Beetles. 2. Beetles—Experiments. 3. Experiments.] I. Kuhn, Dwight, ill. II. Title.
QL576.2.P36   2000   99-053770
595.76—dc21   CIP
                                                                    AC

Note on metric conversions: The metric conversions given in Chapters 2 and 3 of this book are not always exact equivalents of U.S. measures. Instead, they provide a workable quantity for each experiment in metric units. The abbreviations used are:

cm	centimeter	**kg**	kilogram
m	meter	**l**	liter
g	gram	**cc**	cubic centimeter

CONTENTS

1

The Beetle Brigade

If success is measured in numbers, beetles are the insect world's biggest success story. There are more than 350,000 known kinds, or species, of beetles—more kinds than are found in any other group of living things. In fact, one out of every five known species of living things—plant or animal—is a beetle! Ladybugs, click beetles, scarabs, water beetles, weevils, and fireflies are just a few of the many beetle families.

Beetles have been around since the days of the dinosaurs. The oldest recorded beetle fossils are about 250 million years old. Today, beetles of one kind or another live in every part of the world (except Antarctica). There are beetles in forests, deserts, lakes, mountain peaks, farm fields, and backyards everywhere. Some beetles even live in houses. The greatest numbers of beetles, however, are found in tropical regions.

There are more known kinds of beetles than any other living thing on earth.

Beetle Bodies

With so many different species, beetles have an amazing variety of body shapes and sizes. Some, like ladybugs and potato beetles, are round. Others, like fireflies, click beetles, and soldier beetles, are slender. The smallest beetles are tiny fungus beetles that measure barely 1/100 inch (0.25 mm) long. The biggest species are long-horned beetles that live in tropical regions. Some of these giant beetles are more than 6 inches (15 cm) long!

Beetles come in an amazing variety of sizes and shapes. Some bodies are round, like that of the Colorado potato beetle (left). Others are long and slender, like that of the flour beetle (above).

The head of this maple borer beetle includes two antennae, compound eyes, and a pair of clamp-like jaws called mandibles.

Large or small, beetles share certain characteristics. Like all insects, they have six legs and three body segments—head, thorax, and abdomen. A hard outer covering, called the exoskeleton, protects a beetle's body. Like most winged insects, beetles have two pairs of wings. But a beetle's front set of wings is not used for flying. Instead, they form a protective sheath for the hind wings, which do all the work. When a beetle takes off, the wing sheaths (elytra) flip up, and the transparent hind wings unfold.

The coloring of beetles varies as much as their other physical traits. Some beetles—like this tortoise beetle—are colored to blend into their surroundings. Other beetles, like the brightly colored Mexican bean beetle (opposite) use coloring as a warning signal to potential enemies.

Most beetles have two compound eyes, with many facets, or lenses, on each. Antennae, which give beetles their senses of taste and touch, vary widely in size and shape. Most beetles have strong mouthparts, or mandibles, for chewing food.

Beetles vary as much in color as they do in size and shape. Some are dull brown or black, and some are mottled to blend in with their surroundings. Others rank as some of the flashiest members of the insect world, sporting brilliant reds and yellows, and bold spots and stripes. Some beetles even gleam with metallic shades of blue, green, or copper.

Family Members

Beetles can be grouped in families based on body features and other physical traits. For example, many beetles have long snouts, with mouthparts located at the ends. Called snout beetles, this family includes weevils and other beetles that do great damage to plants. Nearly half of all beetles are weevils.

Weevils belong to a group, or family, of beetles that are characterized by long snouts that have mouthparts at the ends. These beetles are called snout beetles.

Ground beetles live in grass, on forest floors, along shores of lakes and streams, and in other areas where tiny insects and other kinds of food are available.

Ground beetles make up another big family. In fact, there are 40,000 different kinds of ground beetles worldwide. As their name suggests, they're found under logs, among stones, along the shores of lakes and streams, and scuttling around in the grass. Depending on the species, these beetles feed on everything from seeds to tiny insects to slugs and snails.

The scarabs form a colorful beetle family with about 35,000 known members. They include june bugs, Japanese beetles, flower beetles, and many others. Many scarabs have large horns that they use during mating contests, to flip their rivals upside-down.

Stag beetles, members of a different group, rank among the strangest-looking insects in the world. Male stag beetles have huge jaws that look like a stag's antlers. The jaws of some stag beetles are as big as their entire bodies! These beetles use their jaws in mating fights to pick up rivals and throw them down.

Click beetles have a special jumping device that helps them survive. It consists of a projection that fits into a socket on the beetle's thorax. If a click beetle is flipped onto its back—a position that leaves most beetles helpless—it flexes the projection and pops up several inches into the air. With luck, the beetle lands right-side up!

Many kinds of water beetles live in ponds and streams. Some glide over the surface in search of prey. Others, such as diving beetles, go underwater to hunt other insects and tiny fish. Diving beetles carry a supply of air on their dives—trapped under their elytra. When the oxygen is used up, the beetle returns to the surface for more air.

Opposite: Japanese beetles are members of the scarab family. Many of these beetles are covered in shiny, metallic colors.
Right: Some water beetles, like this diving beetle larva, go under water to hunt insects, tiny fish, tadpoles, and salamanders.
Inset: This large click beetle is also called an eyed beetle, for obvious reasons.

"BEETLE BULBS"

On warm summer nights, tiny points of light flicker among the trees. The lights are made by fireflies, beetles that have the amazing ability to glow in the dark. Fireflies are among the handful of living things that are bioluminescent—they can produce light.

A firefly has special body chemicals that react with each other to create light. Each firefly species has its own pattern of flashes—some flash once every six seconds, others use two flashes followed by a pause, or some other sequence. They use their lights to find mates. Males fly around flashing their light patterns, while females wait on the ground. When a female sees a male with the same flash pattern as her own, she flashes back.

Firefly larvae, which also produce light, are sometimes called glowworms. In some firefly species, the larvae lose their bioluminescence when they become adults. In the United States, most of the fireflies that produce light as adults live in the eastern part of the country.

Adult firefly

Glowing abdomen of adult

Eggs from a ladybug beetle sit on a leaf.

From Egg to Adult

Beetles go through four life stages—egg, larva, pupa, and adult. This is called complete metamorphosis. After mating, adult females lay eggs in a place where the young will find food when they hatch. They may be deposited on a plant leaf or some other location, depending on the type of beetle and what it eats. Diving beetles lay their eggs in water, and their larvae hatch and live there. Ladybugs will lay their eggs on plants where aphids are found. Aphids are tiny insects that feed on plant juices, and they are the favorite prey of ladybugs.

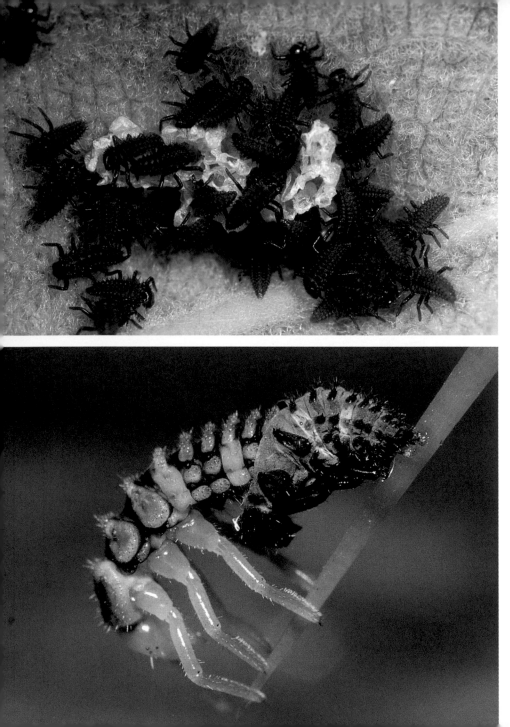

Top: Ladybug larvae look nothing like adults. *Bottom:* As most beetle larvae grow, they shed their skin (molt) to make room for a larger body.

Beetle larvae look nothing like adults. Many look more like little worms and are often called grubs. The larvae start to eat as soon as they hatch.

As it gets bigger, a beetle larva outgrows its skin. It then molts, or sheds its old skin. After molting, it emerges in a new, better-fitting skin. After molting several times, the larva enters the next stage in its life. It sheds its skin once more and becomes a pupa. In this stage, the insect does not eat or move. But its body undergoes great changes. Finally, the pupa's skin, or casing, splits open, and an adult beetle crawls out. Soon it will mate and create offspring that begin the metamorphosis cycle on their own.

While all beetles go through the same life cycle, the time it takes to complete the cycle varies by species. Most beetles complete the cycle from egg to adult within a year. But some beetles may stay in the larval stage for several years. Larvae and pupae also differ in appearance from one beetle species to the next, just as adults do.

Beetle life spans also vary. In cold climates, some beetles hibernate. They find a protected place and spend winter in a dormant state. Ladybugs, for example, spend the winter clustered together under leaves and rocks, or in hollow trees.

When an adult ladybug emerges from its pupa it is yellow. It turns red later in life. *Inset:* In cold climates certain beetles—like the ladybug—will hybernate.

17

Burying beetles are "carrion" beetles. They feed on dead plants and animals. Here, a burying beetle is burying a shrew on which to lay her eggs.

Strange Tastes

As a group, beetles eat just about everything you can think of, and some things you'd probably rather not think of. But different species enjoy different foods. Usually, beetle larvae like to eat the same foods as the adults.

Many beetles eat plant matter—leaves, stems, or fruit. Some will eat only certain types of plants; others are more adaptable. Some beetles eat only mold and fungi. And some, including dung beetles, have very strange tastes. They feed on animal droppings, straining out bits of undigested food, bacteria, and molds. They also store balls of dung underground, placing the balls with their eggs to serve as food for their young when the larvae hatch.

Many types of beetles feed on dead plants and animals. These "carrion" beetles include burying beetles, which lay their eggs on a dead animal and bury them. The dead animal will be food for the larvae when they hatch.

Some beetles depend on other insects in all or some of their life stages. For example, blister beetle larvae live inside bees' nests, where they eat bee eggs and honey until they're ready to pupate. Certain other beetles spend their lives in ants' nests, where the ants feed them.

Ladybugs and tiger beetles are among the many predatory beetles. Ladybugs patrol plants in search of aphids, whiteflies, and other insect prey. Tiger beetles race over the ground to catch other insects in their strong jaws. Tiger beetle larvae can't run very fast. Instead, they build traps—they burrow into the ground and wait, with their jaws open, at the bottom of the hole. When an insect falls in, it's caught in the larva's jaws.

A hungry ladybug larva preys on a group of aphids, its favorite food.

Beetles and their larvae can also become prey for hungry birds, toads, and other predators. Some beetles defend themselves against predators with chemical sprays. When blister beetles are disturbed, they release an irritating chemical that can blister skin. Bombardier beetles can spray a cloud of vile-smelling fluid that makes potential enemies think twice before attacking.

Beetles such as this potato beetle may become food for toads and other animals.

Beetles and People

With their strange forms and colors, beetles have always fascinated people. Beetles were even mentioned in the myths of the ancient Egyptians, who believed that a giant scarab pushed the sun across the sky. The Egyptians were among several ancient peoples who used scarab beetles in jewelry.

Today, beetles are usually thought of as pests. Many kinds of beetles do serious harm to crops, trees, and ornamental plantings. June bug grubs eat plant roots. Wood borer larvae tunnel into trees. Larvae and adult beetles of many kinds attack plant leaves, fruits, and stems.

This june bug grub is feeding on plant roots. Grubs can do serious damage to plants, trees, and crops.

Colorado potato beetles are a serious problem for many American farmers. This beetle has developed the ability to resist many insecticides that farmers use to control pests. Farmers are now turning to other methods of control, including rotating crops and introducing certain spiders and other predators that will kill potato beetles.

Other pests that cause trouble for people are carpet beetles, whose larvae feed on fibers in carpeting. Flour beetles and mealworms (the larvae of darkling beetles) get into stored flour and other grain products. Museum beetles have a specialized diet—they favor the stuffed and preserved animals displayed in natural history museums!

EVIL WEEVILS

In America during the 1800s, cotton was the vital crop in the South. From the Carolinas to Texas, farmers depended on a cash crop of cotton for their living. Then, in 1892, a little beetle called the boll weevil arrived in Texas.

Less than a quarter-inch long, the boll weevil has a huge appetite for cotton. Adults eat buds and blossoms, and then lay their eggs in the bolls, or seed pods, where the cotton fibers develop. Larvae then hatch and eat the cotton fibers. These weevils multiply quickly, producing five to ten generations each year.

Within 30 years of its arrival, the boll weevil had spread through cotton fields across the American South, destroying crops and bankrupting cotton farmers.

In the end, boll weevils brought major changes and improvements to agriculture in the South. Farmers learned that it was too risky to depend on a single crop. As insurance, they began to diversify and grow other crops besides cotton. Those who continued to grow cotton were forced to use chemical pesticides to control boll weevils. Even with pesticides, these insects still do millions of dollars worth of damage each year.

Cotton bud and ball

Adult ladybugs are large consumers of aphids, which are considered to be pests by gardeners and farmers.

Although beetles are thought of as pests, there are many beetles that are helpful to people. Carrion beetles and dung beetles are important members of nature's "clean-up squad." Without them, the world would be a messier place. Consider that a single cow produces about 7 tons of droppings a year!

Ladybugs and other predatory beetles are welcomed by gardeners and farmers because they attack harmful insects. Aphids, for example, can cause serious damage to plants. A single ladybug larva will eat about 400 aphids before it pupates. As an adult, it may eat 5,000 aphids in its lifetime.

2

Collecting and Caring for Beetles

Beetles are great subjects for nature study. Since they live almost everywhere, they're easy to find. Many kinds can be caught and kept for a while, so you can observe them close-up. You can also buy beetles from mail order sources such as those listed on page 46.

You will need to set up a home for your beetles and provide them with food and water. This section will tell you how to do that. When you have finished studying your beetles, release those you captured in the wild. Take them back to the place where you found them. Do not release beetles that you buy through the mail. They may not survive where you live—or they may survive and become pests. Ladybugs are the exception to this rule. They are beneficial insects and may be released just about anywhere.

There are many varieties of beetles, and they live nearly everywhere. Collecting and studying them is quite easy.

Beetle Hunt

Look for beetles in warm weather. Mid- to late summer is the best time to look because there will be plenty of adult beetles around. Take along a container, such as a small jar or a coffee can, with a lid. Punch small holes in the lid so air can get in. Or use netting and a rubber band to cover a container.

The types of beetles you find will depend on where you live and where you look. Check under rocks or fallen tree limbs for ground beetles. Look on stems and leaves for plant-eating types. It won't be long before you find a beetle of one sort or another. Your local library may have an insect guide that will help you identify your beetles and learn more about them. There are also many web sites that provide information for curious beetle collectors.

Many beetles are easy to catch—just scoop them up with your container, and quickly put on the lid. Keeping certain types of beetles for more than a few hours may be difficult, though, depending on what they eat. Beetles that feed on leaves and other plant material are easiest to keep because it's not hard to provide their food. Those that prey on living insects are more difficult. You may not be able to supply them with live food.

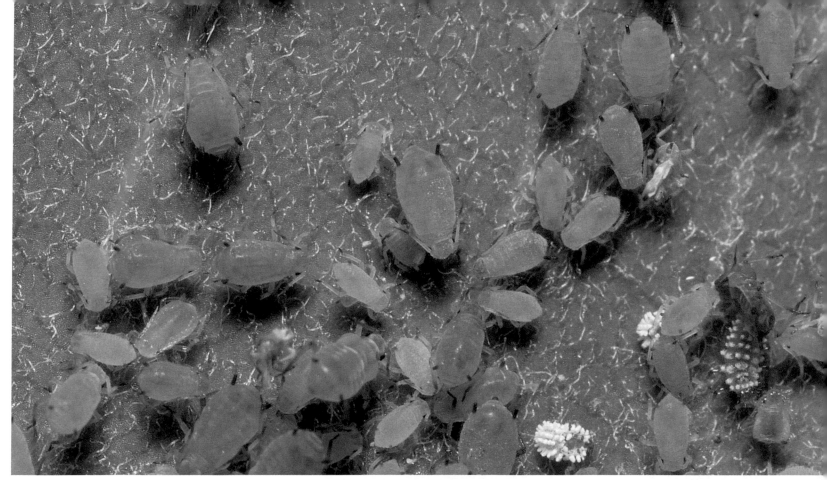

Aphids such as these make good food for captured ladybugs and certain other kinds of beetles.

Your insect guide will help you find out what each beetle eats. Look for clues when you capture beetles, too. For example, if you find beetles on plants, and there are holes in the leaves, the beetles have probably eaten them. Put some of those leaves in the container with your captured beetles. If there are other insects, such as aphids, on the plants, the beetles may eat those insects. You'll need to take along some of the insects to feed them.

Beetles by Mail

Several kinds of beetles can be obtained by mail order, from biological supply houses (see page 46). They include mealworms, which are the larvae of darkling beetles (*Tenebrio*), and flour beetles (*Tribolium,* see photo, page 44). Both types are easy to keep. If you set up a home for these beetles and provide them with food, you can study their entire life cycles. You can also buy mealworms at pet stores, where they are sold as food for fish, lizards, and other animals.

Ladybugs are also available through the mail. Gardeners often buy these beetles by the hundreds and release them among their plants, to control aphids and other insect pests. Ladybugs are more difficult to keep inside however, because they must eat live prey.

Mealworm beetle (*Tenebrio*) larvae (shown below with an adult) are easily ordered from biological supply companies.

Beetle Care

If you want to keep your beetles longer than a day or so, give them a special home. You can use an aquarium, a clear plastic container, or a large jar. Cover the container with mesh, secured by a rubber band. Or punch holes in the jar lid so air can circulate.

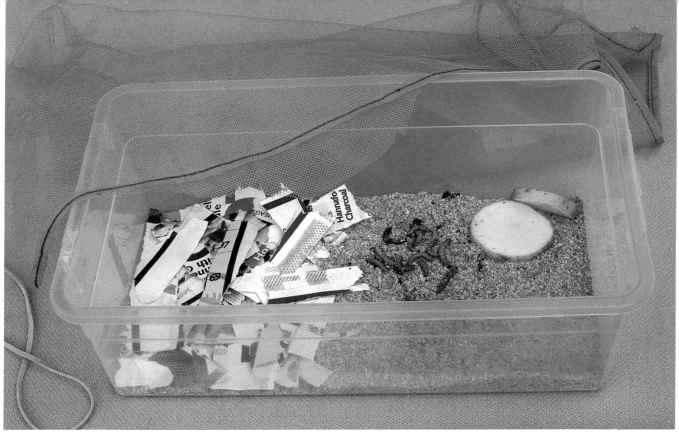

Mealworm beetle homes can be simple.

The beetles will need food and moisture. Here's what to provide:

Wild beetles: Give your beetles fresh food every day. Plant eaters will need a supply of fresh leaves from the type of plant where you found them. Lightly mist the inside of the container with a spray bottle to provide water.

Mealworms: Larvae and adults eat bran. Put a layer of bran about two inches deep in their container. Place a slice of raw potato on top of the bran to provide moisture. Replace the potato every day. A thin layer of shredded paper on top of the bran will give the beetles a place to hide and lay eggs.

Flour beetles need a mix of white flour, whole wheat flour, brewer's yeast, and a potato slice for moisture.

Flour beetles: Flour beetles like a mixture of four parts white flour, four parts whole-wheat flour, and one part brewer's yeast. Put a layer of this mixture about two inches deep in their container. Place a slice of raw potato on top for moisture. Replace the potato piece daily.

Ladybugs: Ladybugs will need aphids. Look for these tiny insects on stems and the undersides of leaves. Check plants where you find ladybugs or ants crawling on stems—ants are often found near aphids. You'll need to look very closely to spot the aphids, which may be green, yellow, orange, purple, or multicolored. When you find them, clip a section of the plant and gently place it, aphids and all, in a covered container. Transfer the clipping and the aphids into your beetle home.

A good ladybug home will require a steady supply of live aphids. Remember: adult ladybugs can eat a lot of aphids in just one day.

3

Investigating Beetles

In the pages that follow, you'll find some activities that will help you learn more about the behaviors and requirements of beetles. Have fun with these activities. Then, when you are done, release wild beetles back into the place where you found them. Remember that beetles you have purchased—except ladybugs—should not be released.

How Many Aphids Does a Ladybug Eat in a Day?

Ladybugs love tasty aphids. Based on what you've read, decide how many aphids you think one ladybug can eat in a day. Then do this activity to see if you are right.

What to Do:

1. To find and collect aphids, follow the instructions in chapter 2, under Beetle Care (page 31). Put some aphid-covered plant clippings in your container. Carefully count how many aphids are on the clippings.
2. Put a ladybug in the jar with the aphids. Cover the jar with netting and secure with a rubber band.
3. Check the container in an hour. Count the aphids that are left.
4. Continue to check the container and count the aphids at intervals during the day. After 24 hours, stop the experiment and release the ladybug.

What You Need:

* Clear container, such as a jar
* Netting
* Rubber band
* Ladybug (adult or larva)
* About 100 aphids

Aphids feed by sucking juices from plant leaves.

Results: Keep a record of your observations. Each time you check the container, write down the time and the number of aphids you see. How many are left at the end?

Conclusions: What do your results tell you about a ladybug's appetite for aphids?

Do Mealworms Become Adults Faster in Warm or Cool Temperatures?

Like all beetle larvae, mealworms grow, pupate, and become adults. How will temperature affect the change from pupa to adult? Make a prediction, and then do this experiment to see if you are right. You can also use flour beetle pupae in this activity.

What You Need:
* Two identical containers
* Netting and rubber bands
* Two room thermometers
* Mealworm pupae

What to Do

1. To get mealworm pupae that are the same age, separate a group of larvae that are all the same size from your main mealworm culture. Place these larvae in a separate mealworm home, set up with food and moisture as explained in Chapter 2 (page 29). When they pupate, they will stop moving and become inactive. Use those that begin to pupate on the same day for this activity.

2. Place an equal number of mealworm pupae in each container. (The pupae don't need food or water.) Cover the containers with netting secured by rubber bands.

Mealworm beetle larvae

Mealworm beetle pupae

3. Put one container in a warm room, but not in direct sunlight. Put the other in a cool place, such as a basement. Set the room thermometers next to the containers. Try to keep conditions other than temperature the same for both containers.

4. Check the containers every day. Record the temperature in each place.

Results: Note which container has adult beetles first. How long after that do adults emerge in the second container?

Conclusions: What do your results tell you about the temperatures and climate in which mealworms thrive?

What You Need:

* Large flat container, such as a plastic food storage box
* Netting and rubber bands
* Darkling or flour beetles
* Possible foods: white flour, wheat bran, sugar, breakfast cereal, salt, wood chips

Which Foods Do Darkling Beetles Like Best?

Darkling beetles (adult mealworms) are pests that can invade stored food. Which foods will they prefer, given a choice? Decide what you think, and then do your own beetle taste test to see if you are right. You can also do this with flour beetles.

What to Do:

1. Place equal amounts of different foods at various locations in the container.
2. Add the beetles. Cover the container with netting, secured by a rubber band. Be sure that light and temperature levels are the same in all parts of the box—make sure it is not brighter or warmer on one side.
3. Check the box in an hour or so to see where the beetles are. Check several more times over the next few hours. Then return the beetles to their home.

Results: Each time you check the box, note how many beetles are at each food pile. Write down your observations.

Conclusions: What did this activity show about beetle food preferences? Try the activity again, using different foods. Or try it with mealworms, to see if the larvae like the same foods as adults.

Darkling beetles are pests that invade stored food.

* Two beetles of the same type and size
* Two small containers, such as paper cups or jars
* Large flat container, such as a food storage box
* Netting and rubber bands
* Graph paper

Do Beetles Move Faster When They're Warm or Cold?

Like all insects, beetles are affected by heat and cold. How does temperature affect the speed at which they move? Make a prediction based on what you know about beetles. Then hold a beetle race to find out.

What to Do:

1. Put a sheet of graph paper in the bottom of the flat container. Cut the paper to fit if necessary.
2. Place each beetle in a container, and cover the tops with netting secured by rubber bands. Put one container in a warm room (but not in direct sunlight). Put the other in the refrigerator.
3. After 15 minutes, take the refrigerated beetle from its container and put it in the center of the graph paper. Count how many squares it crosses in a set amount of time, such as 30 seconds. Return the beetle to your beetle home.
4. Now put the warm beetle on the graph paper. Count the squares it crosses in the same amount of time, and return it to the beetle home.

Results: Which beetle crossed the most squares?
Conclusions: Based on your results, how does temperature affect beetle speed?

Use graph paper to chart the movements of your beetles.

More Activities with Beetles

1. Watch beetles fly outdoors. Place a ladybug or another beetle on the palm of your hand, and blow gently on it. The wing sheaths will pop up, and the beetle will take flight. Follow the beetle as far as you can to see how far it flies.

2. Count firefly flashes. Catch a firefly and place it in a jar, with netting over the top. Put the jar in a dark place and count the number of times the firefly flashes each minute. Is there a pattern to the flashes? Put the container in the refrigerator for 10 to 15 minutes. Then take it out and count the flashes again. Does the pattern change?

3. Follow a ladybug in the garden. Find a ladybug on a plant and watch it as it moves around. Does it travel in a straight line or wander over different parts of the plant? If the ladybug finds aphids or other prey, watch to see how it catches and eats its food.

A ladybug's wing sheaths will rise before the insect takes flight.

You can observe how beetles move by placing them on diferent kinds of surfaces.

4. Check out beetle locomotion. Place an adult beetle on a slippery surface, such as glass or porcelain, and watch it walk. Now put the beetle on a rough surface, such as a piece of wood. Which type of surface does the beetle handle best? Does tilting the surface make a difference?

43

Results and Conclusions

Here are some possible results and conclusions for the activities on pages 33 to 41. Many factors may affect the results of these activities. If your results differ, try to think of reasons why. Repeat the activity with different conditions, and see if your results change.

How Many Aphids Does a Ladybug Eat in a Day?

Your results will vary depending on how hungry, how old, and what species your ladybug is. Some ladybug larvae consume 100 aphids a day.

Do Mealworms Become Adults Faster in Warm or Cool Temperatures?

The pupal stage usually lasts anywhere from 7 to 24 days. Generally, the pupae will mature faster in warm temperatures.

Adult mealworm beetles

Flour beetles consuming fish food pellets.

Which Foods Do Darkling Beetles Like Best?
Your results will depend on the foods you use. Our beetles liked white flour and wheat bran best. They spent a lot of time hiding in the wood chips, but did not eat any.

Do Beetles Move Faster When They're Warm or Cold?
The warm beetle will win the race. Like all insects, beetles are cold-blooded. Chilling a beetle lowers its body temperature and slows down its body processes, including movement.

Some Words About Beetles

Bioluminescent Able to produce light.

Dormant Inactive.

Elytra The wing sheaths of a beetle. They cover and protect the wings when the beetle isn't flying.

Exoskeleton The hard outer skin of an insect. It takes the place of an internal skeleton.

Grubs The larvae of many beetles.

Hibernate To spend winter in a dormant state.

Larvae The young of beetles and other insects.

Pupa Dormant stage during which a larva matures into an adult beetle.

Sources for Beetles and Supplies

You can buy ladybugs, mealworms, and flour beetles through the mail. Except for ladybugs, beetles bought through mail-order sources such as these should not be released into the wild.

Carolina Biological Supply
2700 York Road
Burlington, NC 27215
(800) 334-5551

Connecticut Valley Biological
82 Valley Road, P.o. Box 326
Southampton, MA 01073
(800) 628-7748

Insect Lore
P.O. Box 1535
Shafter, CA 93263
(800) LiveBug

For More Information

Books

Crewe, Sabrina. *The Ladybug* (Life Cycles). New York, NY: Raintree/Steck Vaughn, 1998.

Goor, Ron. Nancy Goor (Contributor). *Insect Metamorphosis: From Egg to Adult.* Old Tappan, NJ: Atheneum, 1990.

Greenaway, Theresa. *Beetles* (Minipets). New York, NY: Raintree/Steck Vaughn, 1999.

Johnson, Sylvia A. *Beetles.* Minneapolis, MN: Lerner, 1982.

Kneidel, Sally Stenhouse. *Creepy Crawlies and the Scientific Method: More Than 100 Hands-On Science Experiments for Children.* Golden, CO: Fulcrum Publishing, 1993.

Kneidel, Sally Stenhouse. *Pet Bugs: A Kid's Guide to Catching and Keeping Touchable Insects.* New York, NY: John Wiley & Sons, 1994.

Kubo, Hidekazu. *Beetles.* Chatham, NJ: Raintree Publications, 1990.

Web Sites

Coleoptera

This international society dedicated to the study of beetles provides beetle news, conservation information, and links to other beetle sites—**www.coleopsoc.org**

Dung Beetles

Everything you ever wanted to know about dung beetles, including information on behavior, identification, and life cycle—**www.insect-world.com/main/dung.html**

The Firefly Files

At this site you will find facts about firefly behavior, habitat, and bioluminescence, as well as ways to attract them to your yard—**iris.biosci.ohio-state.edu/projects/FFiles**

Index

Note: Page numbers in italics indicate pictures.